NEW AND SELECTED POEMS

D0701145

By the same author

Poems
Possible Laughter

Translations
The Odes of Horace
The Poems of Catullus
The Epigrams of Martial
La Fontaine: Selected Fables

NEW AND SELECTED POEMS

James Michie

CHATTO & WINDUS

THE HOGARTH PRESS

LONDON

Published in 1983 by
Chatto & Windus · The Hogarth Press
40 William IV Street
London WC2N 4DF

British Library Cataloguing in Publication Data

Michie, James
    New and selected poems.
    I. Title
    821'.914   PR6063.I/

    ISBN 0-7011-2723-6

This book has been published with subsidy
from the Arts Council of Great Britain.

Printed in Great Britain by
Redwood Burn Ltd
Trowbridge, Wiltshire

To Patrick Kavanagh, in friendship

Author's Note

This volume consists of old as well as new poems. The old poems are those which I have thought most worth preserving from *Possible Laughter*, first published in 1959. A few of them have been very lightly revised.

J.M.

Contents

New Poems

Poems from *Possible Laughter*

NEW POEMS

For Dylan Thomas
Died November 9, 1953

Only Prose was pleased when he was dead
Who housed more music in his bulbous head
Than all the cupolas that have hummed with singers,
And wrung more chimes from his chubby fountain fingers
Than twelve bell-ringers, arms all going together;
Yet made of life such heavy-hearted weather
That neither love nor money kept him warm,
For wherever he slept or drank his pet storm
Of imagination followed him around,
Till it turned rogue and clawed him to the ground.
Unregarded now, like plain girls, are the words
He gave fine moments to, stiff as dead birds
The images he flew to altitudes
Unbreathable before, and solitudes
Again the deserts he drove his rhythms through,
Biblical and furious as Jehu,
Lonely as Rimbaud, crazy as Canute,
In obstinacy and thirst to the absolute
Joy of the last line.
                              When poets die,
Good poems alone, like Loki, refuse to cry;
But the more natural world will always remember
How he toppled from that high week of November
On to his jagged rock. And still we peer
Over the edge for an echo but can hear
Only the surf, see nothing but haze.

Since nobody can pull the ropes of praise
As well as he did for Ann Jones, I've dared
To try to toll for him, finding I cared
More than I thought I could him being dead
Who doesn't care and stays all day in bed.

Proposal

For all that conjuring miles can do
With rosy gauze or a black curtain,
You still seem matter-of-fact and certain;
And, when I remember, you are you
And still not too good to be true.

But if the curving earth is set
On forcing horrible reflections
Of its own hunchback on our affections,
Then let us agree to try to forget
And meet, if again, as we first met.

Nine Times

Nine times worse than abandonment by woman,
Because unappealable, because superhuman,
Is the scorn of the Muses—and rarely the wiser the poorer
Poet. Nine times, too, cooler than Nora
Walking out of her Doll's House of sham
With a flourish of doors is the quite soundless slam
With which inspiration leaves. Back jumps the Sahara,
Bringing the long-faced grasshoppers which are a
Burden, rubbing their legs and making grimaces,
Till paper becomes the parody of an oasis,
A patch of drought in a world of jeering garden.
God knows how those divine girls can harden
Their hearts against the old devoted beaux
Who fucked so boisterously once. God knows
How poetry greys insensibly to prose.

To My Daughter

When I'm far out in drink, your musical box
Gives me the horrors. Mermaids on the rocks,
Beached rabbits, stranded starfish, teddy bears —
Simpering pyknic picnickers in pairs —
To a terrible *rallentando* tinkle pass
Across a thumb-hazed sky of plastic glass.
Then you rewind the sea-song that's run down
And paddle in glee, my darling, while I drown.

Ladies

So, what distinguishes
Ladies from women?
It's not that the others
Are what is called common,
But that ladies are rare.
They can go swimming,

For instance, naked
Without a self-glance,
They can lounge unasked
And content at a dance,
And yet move, and strike,
Like a fer-de-lance.

Ladies tell lies,
But of the best sort,
And they also tell truths
When they're truly caught,
For their credible words
Follow the heart.

When cornered a lady
Never takes cover;
What she *may* take, though,
Is a different lover
Before she's quite thrown
The last one over.

No lady, lastly,
Since the bad world began
Has blamed it on apples
Any more than
Would—if there were one—
A gentleman.

Gentlemen

It didn't have that much to do with class.
I don't believe I'm squinting through a glass
Tinted by age or alcohol, but I swear
There used to be people about who had an air
Of modesty, resolve and openness,
Who did more than they promised and said less
Than you expected—not charm-strangled cadgers,
Tweed-muffled fakes or self-promoted majors,
But soft-voiced, humorous gentlemen. The word
Looks antique, awkward. Nowadays it's heard
On the mouths of auctioneers and mostly seen
In toilets or Appointments by the Queen.
There'll always be heroes, but I miss the panache
Of the quiet man with the unfunny moustache.

Double Blind

When I was young, myopic eyes
Excused me well from seeing decay,
    And as for my demise
    So blurred was the small gap
It seemed unfigurably far away.

Near sight improves? That's not my truth.
I still can't read the big word *die*;
    Worse, don't recall the youth
    With the same handicap
Who never saw me when he waved goodbye.

Our Troops

A lorry-load of soldiers (petrol chokes
The timid evening) puts the road behind,
Red-faced and joking. Let them keep their jokes
Stuck on their faces till they come to find

Laughing unseasonable. They've laughed too much,
Their humour's gone. So, children, please don't cheer,
Don't wave at them, above all do not touch,
Or they might flare up hectically and veer

Backwards. The motive of these loyal flags,
Mindlessly boomeranging, could arrive
To decorate our town with bones and rags
And leave the light the only thing alive.

Discoverer

White and curved as a shell she lies
On the long dune of the bed,
Mother-of-pearl in her nails and eyes;
    In her head
Oceanic themes have stirred
    Through leaning
Galleries sea-meaning
    Without foam of the word.

Who found the shell still hardly breathes
Lest he derange the music. Ear
Flattened against her body's wreaths
    To hear
The pulse of pleasure seized,
    He ponders
Over her name, and wonders
    At woman pleased.

Bad Dada

Charged by the music police
With issuing false notes
The hangdog oboist
Scuttles on tropical ice

Viewed from sofas on cliffs
With raptest inattention
By a superb committee
Of Second Empire stiffs.

Unease! Absence of germs,
Metaphor, weather! But under
The lee of a limp crag
Something of interest squirms,

Ochreous, vermiform —
The sort of birth one's hands
Itch to cram back inside
The raped womb of the norm.

Alone on the Beach

I wish you were here on this long occasion.
Your patient, almost Asian
Application to pleasure
Would have passed the examination—subject: Leisure.

Sun loves the truly lazy, and despises
This fidget who compromises
Between enjoyment and regretting
No work to blight, no you to bless the setting.

Tulips

Lean spiritual hounds on long green leashes,
Violently, soundlessly,
Tulips throng in the house on their intense way somewhere
    else.
Glorious with self-regard, each hard bud bends forward
In an access of concentration
To define pellucidly, to be
Indisputably tulip—
As though, if it relaxed, anyone could make a mistake!

For a week we are the journey, interposed place,
As they run through us
Into ruin and beyond.

They ignore us,
Yet in passing seem to imply a human fault.
Lucky the room used, without acknowledgement,
For their short cut to death.

For a Divorced Friend

Kind person who pulled down
A house that stood in the way
To a rubble of habits, resume
   Your gentle nature
   And grooved day.

Two rooms are your good luck —
Needless to wish you more,
For a wish seems pompous, a flourish
   Like the tick on a sum,
   And anyway your

Right answers will all find you
In the end. So little fuss
Is sure to escape the baboon's
   Intelligence,
   His animus

And viler praise. Since you bribe
Nobody, nobody sounds
The trumpet you don't need to hear.
   You want nothing but love,
   Thousands of pounds

And music. Friends you allow,
But few manage to last,
Their disorderly topicality
   No match for the clean
   Aces of the past.

Leave the door open. May I
Remain one of them who drops
By when a record's playing
   And is noticed with pleasure
   Before it stops?

Frosty Poem

In New York City I wasn't told
That mid-May nights in Vermont can be cold.
Outside, our brook, short of sun
And wind, barely keeps up a run,
Just jogs and limps so as not to freeze;
Flexing her black tender knees,
The mare between the moon and the gate
Crops fiercely as if she couldn't wait
For the calories to turn to heating,
And is blindly warming herself by eating;
Overhead, chipmunks shiver in rows,
Or heaps, or whatever racial pose
Chipmunks adopt; if there were lights,
The woods would be circus-crammed with sights—
Hedgehogs on inchmeal expeditions,
Toads in cool conjugal positions,
Somewhere the bug that bit me lying
Jubilant with my blood and dying,
Jays, if you can imagine it, keeping
Quiet, drops from bathers creeping
Back to huddle inside the lake,
And in the corridors where the snake
Exerts his snakiness unmolested
The hiss and wriggle being rested.
Fur-blanketed, a log fire lit,
I enjoy a comfortable bit
Of fellow-feeling: I can spare
That much for anyone out there.
Indeed, as soon as the next sun breaks
Itself on the farm's edge and makes
A yolky breakfast on my wall
I'll share it gladly with you all.

Message to Geneva

Now that you've gone away
The words creep out to play
And, unafraid of being hurt
By irony however
Tender, content to be small, say
'Yes, I love you with all my heart.'

This spring morning as you wake
To wallpaper and lake
To dance in front of a puritan city
Thawing Switzerland,
I melt with it and want to make
The opposite of an epitaph to your beauty.

Counting the days (like sheep
They jam the gates of sleep),
I've worked at the vulgar sums of hope;
But tomorrow our hearts, colluding
Like a partners' winning trick, will leap
To join on the green table of Europe.

Meanwhile the room looks bare,
And from his dreamy lair
Of picture-frame the painter's lion
Surveys a bed as big
As the old California, where
Our imagination is staked by the million,

And quizzes a moody man
Who hasn't any plan
But to study clocks ticking and striking,
Read weather, and solve
As decipherably as he can
The cloud lines of your forehead, making

The terror of happiness
Dog you less and less
Till it loses the scent, and the fear of words
Cower and turn tail,
So that with any casual guess
You can baffle the sphinxes along your roads.

My mind goes running wild
Over the skyline, to a child
That might land like a picnicker on our shore.
I write this quickly down
Before we meet and my self-styled
Pride shuts its never-locked door.

Biography

Though he lacked the true vocation, undeterred
He stuck to what he had chosen — a hedonist
Who crouched all night in the park but somehow missed
       Catching a wild bird.

At first how many tame geese he misled!
With the furious ingenuity of a Zeus
Condescending to swans, he used to seduce
       Dozens in the reed-bed.

Then the trick failed him, at an earlier age
Than he expected. Now he mounts a show
Of altruism; yet if you were to blow
       Your nose clumsily he'd rage

Inwardly. That he 'cares' he has often told
Himself, and proved it by weeping at Great Art.
But the unkempt tragedies of the next-door heart
       Find him tidy and old —

Old but still much more alive than dead.
He might say, 'I have feelings that you cannot guess.'
That would make us like him even less,
       So he looks it but leaves it unsaid.

Midas

Once the cheap thrill was over—
Turning parrots to brooches, jaundicing geraniums,
Freezing, baroquely, fountains—
He doomed his friends as he met them and, clutching statues,
Became appalled.
Soon, in a world too valuable, he pawed
Each day to death, and then regretfully
Was again the next one's murderer and chief mourner.
By now his future
Smelt of the sultry sweetness of the past.
Even after he'd learnt not to touch,
When he mixed with his people
They moved stiffly — 'The king
Gives us a minute like a vase, but we dread
To shatter it' —and made their best excuses.

Observation

Walking to our respective graves
In superb weather,
I trailed a young duke across Green Park.
The trousers made some difference. All the same,
The conclusion to which I came
Was either rich or stark:
By the way his hands were locked together
I knew we were both slaves.

Ago

Midnight at our backs and fifteen milestones
slumped exhausted by the way,
we walked into Dorset while the moon, reeling,
glowered the colour of barley
and each star was quite distinct.
Then my friend, who was mad and given to understatement,
paused by nettles and a gate and
between the fall of his hair and the bowl of his fingers
struck a match.
Detonation. Hush.
As a raindrop sprints on a pane
a hare poured flat-eared along the lit meadow—
but not in fear.

Romantic Experiment

In the slovenly laboratory we call
Society sometimes a poet will crawl —
Great big unsupervised baby — up the wall
And from a bottle on the topmost shelf
Marked *Danger, Do Not Touch*, or *Self*,
Swallow, and in the slow paralysis
And death that follow scrawl
In blood, vomit or piss:
'God damn you all,
God bless you too — but don't drink this.'

Doreen

All day, apart, she bakes
Nude flesh. With what intent?
That those who make mistakes
Should fancy it was meant

For what, by God, it's not.
Sun-tanned and cold to us,
But to herself the hot
Sister of Narcissus,

All night, alone, Doreen
Muffles her sex with cloth,
Hostess to the unseen
And cunnimordant moth.

Good Morning, Good Evening

My big soft duchess with the housemaid's hands
That feather-duster from my cornered mind
A generation of dead moths and send
Butterflies blooming down my spine — hallo.

My hard oracular peasant who understands
That we can see each other best when blind
And that a silence need not have an end
And that a quarrel is a pause — hullo.

My cloud, my dromedary, who crossed the sands
With rain and rescue when I was resigned
To throat-constricting irony, best friend,
Whore, mother, sister, daughter, queen — hello.

There are three teasing and adoring greetings,
Variously spelled to signify
The vivid differences among our meetings,
Not the dead sameness when we say goodbye.

The Pacifists

Since we're insipid haters
And so hate to have a fight,
How come that overnight
We wake to such ugly craters
In our small lawn? Mole-spite?
No, *we* are the perpetrators

Of damage. When it's too hard
To communicate by signs,
We sow unwitting mines
And snoringly bombard
Our own quivering lines
While sleep is changing guard.

Yet if other, actual tanks
And guns (for which I half pray)
Were to point at us both in broad day,
We might perhaps give thanks
To have found a military way
To surrender, or close ranks.

Hopeful Lies

The lies we tell are only hopes
With kinks in them like periscopes:
When we're submerged and all at sea,
They aim at visibility
Over the choppy interval, and
With luck offer a glimpse of land.

The Last Wasp

When light dims to an early blur
    Which makes me dream I'm going blind;
When the last wasp, colourless fur,
    Blends with the carpet; when I find
Soles chilled by linoleum, the moon
    Rotten and low, and bonfire smoke
Perplexing the late afternoon
    With tears that irrigate and choke;
When mist with mortuary breath
    Doodles on windows notes for death;

When with a histrionic sigh
    The year turns its face to the wall
Of winter and pretends to die,
    Then is the time I like to call
Its bluff, and either counter-attack
    By rushing into love and work,
Or take the long, muddy slog back
    Through memory. Either way, the jerk
Of one or the other blistering rope
    Tightens and lifts some flag of hope.

POEMS FROM *POSSIBLE LAUGHTER*

Quiet, Child

My cry-baby indignation,
    House is empty, parents out.
Too late now to raise a protest.
    Nobody can hear the shout
Little angry injured persons
    Utter under history's clout.

Underneath mad hands of barbers,
    Helpless, sheeted like the dead,
Here we sit and watch the lather
    Tinge alarmingly with red,
And wonder if as well as whiskers
    Experts will remove the head.

The impotent like pills, the nervy
    Swallow war like benzedrine;
The mechanically minded
    Get mashed inside their own machine;
Even the Epicurean porker
    Turns a Christian Gadarene.

Finding water will not flow, the
    Gun-shy spirit leaves the eye,
And the tongue within its burrow
    Dies in arsenic of the lie,
And the trunk of being rots which
    Means and stands as straight as I.

Glumly we chew on with murder
    Long past the appetite of hate.
Nothing but their shadows' outlines
    Left, like grease-stains on a plate,
People leaning over bridges
    Quietly evaporate.

And big as a telephone directory
　　His bomber's casualty list,
Gloved, the pilot leaves behind him,
　　Represented by a mist,
Individuals who were furious,
　　But no longer now exist.

Hush, my infant indignation,
　　We must keep quiet, you and I,
Or someone will report our lively
　　Howling. Members must be sly
In the small and banned society —
　　Those who do not want to die.

For a Friend in the Country

God knows how you find yourself so entertaining!
My hollow places fill with momentary envy
Seeing how one with so many Furies can be
Perpetually refreshed by himself. The same thing

Would drive me mad; for long ago detecting
Nothing, I gave up the search for myself sadly:
The apple which longed for a stone accepted a medley
Of pips in the end, a dozen selves, all acting,

And came to terms with its heart. But, like your spring,
You listen to yourself, certain of your identity,
And talk to yourself with no horror of aridity,
Exchanging unambiguous whispering.

Diaries, old letters, long walks and daydreaming,
Addressing oneself or persons imaginary —
The vulture that feeds on others is your kept canary.
Courageous townsmen run away exclaiming

With terror at your pastimes. The cedar waxwing
Perches at evening. You watch it through binoculars
With a horse and dog like the ones on calendars.
God knows how you find the company so relaxing!

The End of the Sage

At the end of his time the sage
Became light like a balloon.
They thought him mad
For dancing and saying hurrah
With the small voice he had.
Queer in a prisoner of that age.

'Much wiser and much dafter,
Now that I quite agree
To become dead,
I achieve a witticism,
And I see at last,' he said,
'Hazy like foothills possible laughter.'

Before the young guard's gun
Could beat sense back into
A head so light,
Fooling his tormentors
That old man died outright,
Silencing, falling flat like a pun.

The Robin and the Lark

Tail like a painful splinter,
Sham blood running down his chest,
Robin makes the best
Of begging, and with 'Oh sir' 'Please sir' acts
Orphan all winter.

Type of the time-server, he thieves
By a trick of doleful pertinacity
Housemaid's pity,
Picturesque bread and water, but does not see
That the world disbelieves.

And feathers his nest better
Than true outcasts, unheard sufferers,
Since man prefers
To miserable thanks in charity
Cheerfulness from the debtor.

Yet forfeits by the stratagem
The larger adulthood of larks,
Who set up marks
Too high for themselves, and are frozen flying;
Odes are for them,

Death, like a cold comet,
Falling and failure. Robin, at home
With pram wheel, garden gnome,
Is nursery-rhymed, and, limed with children's praise,
Cannot fly from it.

Rhyme Rude to My Pride

O my intolerable
Pride, the rebel
Cain to my Abel,
My life-long trouble,
My hump, my double,
My Siamese growth,
You are destroying us both
By the enormity
Of your deformity.
Have some pity
For both of our sakes!
Look how your arrogance takes
Us far from friends
Down the long dead-ends
No one defends,
Up cul-de-sacs
To fight (with our backs
To a wall of error
And one eye on the mirror)
The spuriously stoical,
Thick-headedly heroical,
Stiff-neckedly moral
Lost cause of a quarrel
That you've picked with life.
As with a mad wife
Uncontrollable
In the street or at table,
For your sordid
Sake I'm avoided.
Even at your best,
Elegantly dressed
In ideals, you're inhuman
Like a fashion woman

Whose silly cult
Of the different and difficult
Is a general insult.
In your noble attitudes
I suspect worse platitudes
Than the ones you escape.
In your monkish shape,
My mesmeric twin,
I see Rasputin
Making my foolish czar
Of a heart unpopular
With the uneducated,
The by now infuriated
Loves and Simplicities.
Worse than all this, it is
You who have stalked away,
Muttering 'cliché',
From morals and money
And matrimony
And each kind ceremony
Of life. Yes, I see
You have tricked me up a tree
To observe mankind,
And now too late I find
That the high-minded
Look blue-behinded
From below, from above
Quaint to the glance of love.
O cacodaemon,
Ingrowing Timon,
Puritanical
Mask, manacle,
Tumour, since no one can
Ever trepan
Us into one man,
And since, if we tried
To commit suicide,
You, my Pride,
Would be too proud and I'd
Be too terrified,

Let us therefore decide
To stand side by side
Without meum or tuum.
For example, this poem
Is as hopelessly ours
As the stones and the flowers
And the people who throw 'em.

Be a Bear

Shaking a box marked 'Please
Support our organised mess',
The approachers are not given
The opposite of yes,

Except where in dark rooms
The uncharitable live,
Developing their own lights
From a repeated negative —

Right, if you like, as saints,
Blind, if you'd rather, as moles,
When the thunder-clap invites
They shake and head-shake in their holes,

While better-minded beasts,
Too civil to refuse,
Gregariously add
To the weeping and the news.

Lion

Lion with the face of God
Hid in a cloud of hair,
Walking worried and just,
Making of captivity
A fabulous desert of pride.

Heraldic, self-possessed
Lion serious as pain,
Yellow as topaz, erupting
Out of a bleak field
Into our imagination.

Sand-throated lion in the glare,
Swamp lion howling, winter lion
Guarding a sunny pose
Even in the east wind.
Lion dreamt or seen in cloud.

King lion with no people,
Roaring enough to shake
Leaves, if there were, from trees,
Breaking and so making
Silence, portentous, alone.

Park Concert

Astounding the bucolic grass,
The bandsmen sweat in golds and reds
And put their zeal into the brass.
A glorious flustered major heads

Their sort of stationary charge.
Their lips are pursed, their cheeks get pink;
The instruments are very large
Through which they render Humperdinck.

The sailors and the parlourmaids
Both vote the music jolly good,
But do not worry if it fades
As they stroll deeper in the wood

Where twenty French horns wouldn't stir
A leaf. The intrepid band try not
To mind the applause (as though it were
A testing fusillade of shot),

Polish their mouthpieces and cough,
Then throw their shoulders back to play
A Pomeranian march. They're off!
And Sousa scares the tits away.

Pan

He touched me among
Secluded pines,
Rooted my tongue
And shook my bones.
Like Atlas, my back
Felt the cleansing storms,
Sensations of rivers
Purged my arms,
And, with the worms,
Where the dead raise barrows
Struggling to get free,
I ate, and the marrow
Magnified me.
As, meeting in a passage,
Two halt at loss,
Time stood before me
But could not pass.
Not a minim of wind
Lay in the scales.
My eye perceived
The racing snails
Among green pillars,
And marked the stages
Of the falling cone;
From the hills' hid cellars
Sulphurous truths
Burned on the ridges
As I came for the first time
Into my own.
Shedding my ruins
Like a winter snake,
Terrified, laughing
For my new skin's sake,
I felt in my chest
A hardening stone,
Then knew that my enemies
Could nail me down
Twenty times, but I

Would get up again,
Compact and alone,
The unslayable man.

Arizona Nature Myth

Up in the heavenly saloon
Sheriff sun and rustler moon
Gamble, stuck in the sheriff's mouth
The fag end of an afternoon.

There in the bad town of the sky
Sheriff, nervy, wonders why
He's let himself wander so far West
On his own; he looks with a smoky eye

At the rustler opposite turning white,
Lays down a king for Law, sits tight
Bluffing. On it that crooked moon
Plays an ace and shoots for the light.

Spurs, badge and uniform red,
(It looks like blood, but he's shamming dead),
Down drops the marshal, and under cover
Crawls out dogwise, ducking his head.

But Law that don't get its man ain't Law.
Next day, faster on the draw,
Sheriff creeping up from the other side
Blazes his way in through the back door.

But moon's not there. He's ridden out on
A galloping phenomenon,
A wonder horse, quick as light.
Moon's left town. Moon's clean gone.

The Nostalgist

His is the house where everything
    Jumps up like a labrador,
And, trying to greet him, drags him sadly
    And intently to the floor.

A jack of clubs in a dark drawer
    Gives him a fright;
Glass paperweights howling with snow
    Gulp him inside.

Army in perpetual retreat,
    His thoughts going over old ground
Cannot disguise disgrace by wearing
    Their boots the wrong way round.

From cups and jugs grim little Lars
    Pick at his heart
Like a banjo, or, accordionists,
    Squeeze out old times.

On step and rail the sunbeams slyly
    Hint at somewhere else.
So many things to slip on and tumble
    Down staircases, down years . . .

The worst room contains a bed,
    Love-letters, skates,
Maps with a rosy India, dead
    Fox-trots, and him.

Delos: Alcaics

'According to the Hymn of Homer, the wandering Latona took refuge
at Delos, where she gave birth to Apollo. . . . The Emperor Julian, we
are told, consulted the oracle, with some degree of affectation, in A.D.
363' (*Blue Guide*).

Men really tried here, harder than ever, but
Again achieved just wilderness, suicide.
    Reptiles, a failed race too, look up at
        Columns they once could have overshadowed.

Where gods are born, men suffer most, leading or
Led. Here a strong man, oracle-mongering
    En route for those bad lands of Persia,
        Wasted a bit of the breath he lost there.

Heat calmly holds; sea-colour immutable
Also. The flies with sunset to live till, the
    Tourists, their prospects stretching further,
        Hover excitedly round the spots where

Most blood was let out, leaving behind them the
Hairpins and coins whence other intelligence
    (Wave paler, sun less red) will guess at
        Date of disaster and end of effort.

On the Death of 2nd Lieutenant Browne

Archetype of all we sensed
We had gone to war against,
Browne and his few wits
Parted, blown to bits.

Though now less lively,
Just as unlovely
As when sound of limb,
His men dispose of him,

And, turning snobbish, burn
With shame to have had to learn
Death at the same school
As the lout and the fool.

A History

Above, flowered colossal voices.
I pushed my way through the stalks,
Thankful for being hidden
From God and the bad hawks.

One day the noise bent down,
A savage-looking bloom;
So I put my head in my hands
And lived in that shuttered room

Where the four doors opened
North south east and west
Over sheer drops, and the windows
Shivered when they were undressed.

To celebrate my safety
And to make doubly sure
Of my strength, I made my fists
Bleed on the furniture,

Then descended, afraid of myself,
Moodily outside,
Where owing to my neglect
The giant flowers had died.

Their booming inaudible,
Each face, a withered shred,
Lay limply. I stood
Alive inspecting the dead.

Alone on the scythed plain,
Aghast at solitude, I knelt
Praying for a single tree
On which to hang my guilt.

Then a creature came from nowhere
And took the crimes from my hands
And hung them all over herself
Like necklaces or armbands.

We shook each other to force
The extremity of love
And raved, but the words rising
Would not marry above.

'I was not looking for you.'
'And I did not want to be found.'
Turning to prefer desert,
We saw our two wrists were bound.

Nightmare

Panicking alone in chloroform
The child awaking, when the fire is
Weak as a jelly and barely warm,
Calls, but sees in its parent's iris
Equal alarm, and so begins to cry
For solider reassurance than a worried eye.

And finds, since sympathy only shelves
Skeletons into cupboards deeper
And comforters talk to cure themselves,
The waker must walk as alone as the sleeper;
Pains are not charmed by visitors in furs,
Nor devils conjured out by passionate amateurs.

Goodbye

The wrongly married drive off
To applause, for everyone feels
Envy for those taking corners,
Even if on three wheels.

Embarking regiments
In two minds sing,
Glad to go but sorry
To reach the campaigning;

And the dots on the deck, growing smaller,
Feel larger with relief
As the thrill of mere movement
Dissipates mere grief.

O airports, tops of trees,
Ships' sirens, platform bells,
Blonde hair flying beside
Motor-gloved farewells —

Whatever else begins
Some obligation ends.
So, passenger and well-wisher,
Wave cheerfully at bends.

I Like You But . . .

I like you but lie to you all, and you never guess.
'There goes,' you say, 'one of the frank. Not a bit
Shy of old dishonour or abashed to confess
What others blush to dissemble, he will sit
In the bar with us, his heart on his sleeve.' Yes,
But jackdaws only jar their beaks on it.

What I said to her about love, or she to me,
Is all for your hearing, and my drunk eye waters
With sentiment, for I can afford to be
Confidential, who make you into porters
To take loads off my mind. No secrecy
Is half so safe as publishing three-quarters.

That way nothing is left to be inferred
From my silence, and you reward me for my showing
What costs me nothing. O jackdaw world, poor bird
To know only what I like to think of you knowing,
And to take that nailed-up weathercock, my word,
As a sign of the wind, whichever way it's blowing!

The Deserter

He ran away anywhere, till the dream
That had trailed him waking was lost. A stream
Stumbled and caught itself and ran
Perfectly on. Peace began.

He lay on his coat on top of a hill,
Useless, while he felt his will
Bleed away and in his head
Neutral liquid well instead —

White internal tears of the brain,
Such as, after weeks of pain,
Clear-headed past belief,
Invalids let fall in relief.

Then felt half happy to be shot,
And fell asleep and quite forgot
What it was that had made him run away:
Not fear, but a frenzy to disobey.

Dooley is a Traitor

'So then you won't fight?'
'Yes, your Honour,' I said, 'that's right.'
'Now is it that you simply aren't willing,
Or have you a fundamental moral objection to killing?'
Says the judge, blowing his nose
And making his words stand to attention in long rows.
I stand to attention too, but with half a grin
(In my time I've done a good many in).
'No objection at all, sir,' I said.
'There's deal of the world I'd rather see dead—
Such as Johnny Stubbs or Fred Settle or my last landlord,
        Mr Syme.
Give me a gun and your blessing, your Honour, and I'll be
        killing them all the time.
But my conscience says a clear no
To killing a crowd of gentlemen I don't know.
Why, I'd as soon think of killing a worshipful judge,
High-court, like yourself (against whom, God knows, I've got
        no grudge—
So far), as murder a heap of foreign folk.
If you've got no grudge, you've got no joke
To laugh at after.'
                        Now the words never come flowing
Proper for me till I get the old pipe going.
And just as I was poking
Down baccy, the judge looks up sharp with 'No smoking,
Mr Dooley. We're not fighting this war for fun.
And we want a clearer reason why you refuse to carry a gun.
This war is not a personal feud, it's a fight
Against wrong ideas on behalf of the Right.
Mr Dooley, won't you help to destroy evil ideas?'
'Ah, your Honour, here's
The tragedy,' I said. 'I'm not a man of the mind.
I couldn't find it in my heart to be unkind
To an idea. I wouldn't know one if I saw one. I haven't one
        of my own.
So I'd best be leaving other people's alone.'
'Indeed,' he sneers at me, 'this defence is

Curious for someone with convictions in two senses.
A criminal invokes conscience to his aid
To support an individual withdrawal from a communal
    crusade
Sanctioned by God, led by the Church, against a godless,
    churchless nation!'
I asked his Honour for a translation.
'You talk of conscience,' he said. 'What do you know of the
    Christian creed?'
'Nothing, sir, except what I can read.
That's the most you can hope for from us jail-birds.
I just open the Book here and there and look at the words.
And I find when the Lord himself misliked an evil notion
He turned it into a pig and drove it squealing over a cliff into
    the ocean,
And the loony ran away
And lived to think another day.
There was a clean job done and no blood shed!
Everybody happy and forty wicked thoughts drowned dead.
A neat and Christian murder. None of your mad slaughter
Throwing away the brains with the blood and the baby with
    the bathwater.
Now I look at the war as a sportsman. It's a matter of
    choosing
The decentest way of losing.
Heads or tails, losers or winners,
We all lose, we're all damned sinners.
And I'd rather be with the poor cold people at the wall that's
    shot
Than the bloody guilty devils in the firing-line, in Hell and
    keeping hot.'
'But what right, Dooley, what right,' he cried,
'Have you to say the Lord is on your side?'
'That's a dirty crooked question,' back I roared.
'I said not the Lord was on my side, but I was on the side of
    the Lord.'
Then he was up at me and shouting,
But by and by he calms: 'Now we're not doubting
Your sincerity, Dooley, only your arguments,
Which don't make sense.'

('Hullo,' I thought, 'that's the wrong way round.
I may be skylarking a bit, but my brainpan's sound.')
Then biting his nail and sugaring his words sweet:
'Keep your head, Mr Dooley. Religion is clearly not up your
        street.
But let me ask you as a plain patriotic fellow
Whether you'd stand there so smug and yellow
If the foe were attacking your own dear sister.'
'I'd knock their brains out, mister,
On the floor,' I said. 'There,' he says kindly, 'I knew you
        were no pacifist.
It's your straight duty as a man to enlist.
The enemy is at the door.' You could have downed
Me with a feather. 'Where?' I gasp, looking round.
'Not this door,' he says angered. 'Don't play the clown.
But they're two thousand miles away planning to do us
        down.
Why, the news is full of the deeds of those murderers and
        rapers.'
'Your Eminence,' I said, 'my father told me never to believe
        the papers
But to go by my eyes,
And at two thousand miles the poor things can't tell truth
        from lies.'
His fearful spectacles glittered like the moon: 'For the last
        time what right
Has a man like you to refuse to fight?'
'More right,' I said, 'than you.
You've never murdered a man, so you don't know what it is
        I won't do.
I've done it in good hot blood, so haven't I the right to make
        bold
To declare that I shan't do it in cold?'
Then the judge rises in a great rage
And writes *Dooley is a Traitor* in black upon a page
And tells me I must die.
'What, me?' says I.
'If you still won't fight.'
'Well, yes, your Honour,' I said, 'that's right.'

57

Alice, My Servant in Jamaica

Alice among the ducks at the garden bottom
With mucky words knows how to curse eggs
Blue and nourishing for a breakfast from them.
And higgledy-piggledy the devoted necks
Worship in gabble her wicked figure down
By the duckpond. Unlike all her sex,
She can wipe a mirror and not look at her own
Reflection, and pick up long-legged insects.

To her department of the beeswaxed floors,
Vine-drilled veranda, shining door-handles,
The daily dignified ambassadors
Through vegetable squalor upon mineral splendour
Of official bicycles ride out to surrender
In a sack the town's citadel of scandals.

At Any Rate

'He's dead,' they shouted as he left his motorbike
And catapulted twenty foot through air
And dented earth. They wanted him to be dead
Out of a sort of innocent malignance
And being born dramatists the lot of them.
And dead he was in the end. The blood gushed
From his ears. 'He's dead,' they told the doctor,
Though he wasn't, as the doctor saw at once,
By any means dead. 'Officer,' they said, 'he's dead.
He ought to be, at any rate if he's human.'
And in the end they were right, dead right.
An hour later, by the tangled bike
(Considered by the crowd by no means done for)
They were still standing, very much alive—
As they ought to be, at any rate if they're human.

Three Dreams

1

Hair long, cheekbones high,
Unencumbered by manners, though clothed in the costume
    of an age,
I meet you, have always known you, used cunning and knives
    to win you in primitive epochs and other lives,
Woman with a tinge of African or Spanish.
We give no sign of recognition, I single you out at parties, we
    face each other at crossroads, I swim round a headland
    and there you are on the beach, conscious of me,
Eyes wide open.
You swerve aside. I follow,
Tracking you through the old.familiar wilderness,
Unhurried because there is no time, unanxious because I am
    sure to find you
Under the oak or catch you under the sea,
In sympathy unlike human sympathy, which is mixed with a
    grain of contempt,
With love not made a lie by the pert desire for discovery,
With love we do not need to name.

2

I see islands floating unknowingly on to the bows of foreign
    ships and sunk
(Gone the name of the archipelago),
The wading ashore, the scuffle in the shallows or the cliffside
    barrage;
The chief consults unruffled, trusting in the local science
And the latest modifications in the arrow.
His sons are soon dead. The women go to the mountain.
High above the sea-shore vegetation flies the morbid, multi-
    coloured flag.

I see the Roman in Bavaria
Baffled by the fir-devils, the miles of fir, the sneering ravens;
The Spaniard breathing with difficulty in Peru,
Or afraid, for fear of laughter, to skate on the Dutch canals.
The Hawaiian turns his face away from me, dying of the
    imported germ.
Crete swarms with a new shape of head,
Makers of the prettiest daggers the Minoans are astonished,
    killed to a man.

Wandering I visit the last Carib lying in a corner, the lost
    Etruscans,
And empty of Red Indians the cheerless plains.

   3
The Siberian tiger sits on a crag of snow
Casting a blue shadow bigger than himself
And destroys with his mouth the appealing, flying deer.
I too tear the haunches and eat the strings and the guts,
The glance of the victim still upon me.
Only I know the true wickedness of the tiger.
His whiskers and eye compel me. I must scurry to please
    him.

The sunny lawn is littered with deadly snakes,
Walk as warily as you may, you are bound to wake them.
Aimed elsewhere my sole treads on the slumbering ribbon,
My shoe squelches the puff adder, the mamba strikes through
    my leggings,
All around alarm of tongues, coilings, ill colours, outrage,
    directed malice,
Till I fall on the sunny lawn, a small Laocöon.

In a gap in the forest I come upon the lion and the wolf
Fighting to the death, the lion losing,
His face gory, righteous, amazed.

He is the king. He has no right to lose.
But the wolf, who is guilty of winning, with a long clever
look
Tears down the lion.
Hiding in a tree,
I love the wolf for this unnatural revolt.

But I am seen. Suddenly a crowd assembles,
Inflamed country faces, farmers with their sons and dogs,
Their pursuit ponderous, full of apparatus.
Running, never quite flying,
Weak I watch my webbed prints in the wet sand recede
behind me.
I kiss the befriending trees, I confide in the river, the currents
are on my side,
Storming through legs, assisting speed.
Perfect my hiding-place in the reeds till each time by chance
discovered.
From deep in the mud-bank they haul me out straining to use
my wings,
For spying to be done to death with sticks.

Girls' School

Bound by a bell's sound, the prayer, the quarrel, the test
Cannot assume capital letters and monomaniacal
Adult faces. The perfunctory is best

For young girls, who will learn the way far too soon
To put all their eggs in one basket, all the heart in a look,
And curse specialization under a later moon.

But now in the milky dormitories they sleep without fuss
Because it is the time for it; as happy to lie by night
Under a quilt as by day on a chequered syllabus.

The hours, pretending they don't know how to combine,
Walk up as charming freebooters, unarmed, disclaiming
Allegiance to that remote and iron-grey battle-line.

Around, the lavatories, the tennis courts and the tinny
Pianos gather initials. Vanishing in a whisper
Or on a piece of paper crumpled in the spinney,

Love is too temporary to be right or wrong.
Somewhere the staff functions, but vaguely, like a hand
Reaching over the gramophone to alter the song

Or prevent the needle sticking in a sentimental groove.
In dreamlike crocodiles they think impregnable or lonely
Perambulations or cotton crowds, listless the girls move

To their first continuous event, the stream the mists cover,
Which is waiting to call Ophelia those who will find it
A flood their love or terror can never get over.

Hand in Hand

Through the neat glade, a disgusting
Bird on every twig,
Two stroll defiantly trusting
That the forest is simple and big.
But eyes in the boles
Have marked them, and, suggesting urinals,
A susurrus breaks from the leaves of the fig.

They may hold like amulets
Precious hands, or go linking
Arms, but no one gets
Cleanly through without slinking.
Quite innocent,
Loving to kiss, although they hadn't meant
It, they find themselves archly winking.

On every branch a sparrow,
An eye in every bark
Shooting a heartless arrow
With initials to its mark.
Bleeding, love turns
To share the doom of the beast that learns
Africa is an amusement park.

Closing Time

Jerusalem Street and Paradise Square
Drive their drinkers home to bed.
Dreaming of fancy houses where
The sheets are white and the lanterns red,
Drunkards grouped round the baby grand
With moonlike face and waving hand
Leave. The seedy last who lingers
Through the tankard sees his fingers.

Turned out in boastful threes and twos,
The champions at darts and soccer
Have hearts that sink into the shoes
That lead them back towards the knocker,
Kick stones, throw sticks dejectedly,
And whistle disconnectedly.
And, as they think about their wives,
The rain returns into their lives.